OPERATION TIMOTHY
GLOBAL

BOOK ONE | *Life Questions*

OPERATION TIMOTHY
BOOK ONE | LIFE QUESTIONS
Copyright © 2024 by CBMC, Inc.

Published in the United States by CBMC, Inc.

CBMC.

All Rights Reserved including translation. No part of this publication may be reproduced, distributed, or transmitted in any form or by any means, including photocopying, recording, or other electronic or mechanical methods, without the prior written permission of the publisher/author, except in the case of brief quotations embodied in reviews and certain other noncommercial uses permitted by copyright law.
Direct requests for permission to
CBMC, P.O. Box 8009, Chattanooga, TN 37414-0009
www.cbmc.com

All Scripture quotations, unless otherwise indicated, are taken from the Holy Bible, New International Version® NIV®
Copyright © 1973, 1978, 1984, 2011 by Biblica, Inc.
Used with permission. All rights reserved worldwide.

ISBN: 978-1-947457-33-1 (softcover)

1st Edition

Printed in the United States of America.

CBMC is Christian Business Mens Connection

FREE — SCAN FOR YOUR OPERATION TIMOTHY MEMORY VERSE KIT

OPERATION TIMOTHY

BOOK ONE

Life Questions

Chapter 1: **WHAT IS THE PURPOSE OF LIFE?**   1

Chapter 2: **IS THE BIBLE CREDIBLE?**   15

Chapter 3: **WHERE IS GOD?**   31

Chapter 4: **WHO IS JESUS?**   47

Chapter 5: **WHY DID JESUS COME?**   59

Chapter 6: **CAN I BE ACCEPTED AND FORGIVEN?**   73

Chapter 1: What is the Purpose of Life?

What if you were born to live for something big? Something more fulfilling than what pulls most people out of bed each morning. Something far more fascinating than the daily discipline imposed by your morning alarm, whether that be your iPhone or a baby crying. Something more satisfying than your income, however substantial that may be. Something worth all of your life, not just the eight-plus hours of the day you devote to your career. Something more compelling than the products marketed by the commercials on TV.

What if you were born to live for something so central it works its way into every answer to every important question you'll ever ask?

What wakes you up every morning and motivates you to press on? Could you define your purpose for being here? Right now? Right here? And, if you could, what size and shape is that purpose? Is it so small it fits only the boundaries of your own life, or is it so large you're still discovering its dimensions?

— Some Say —

"He who has a why to live for can bear with almost any how."
FRIEDRICH NIETZSHE, *German Philospher*

"Everything—a horse, a vine—is created for some duty... For what task, then, were you yourself created? A man's true delight is to do the things he was made for."
MARCUS AURELIUS, *Roman Emperor*

"How strange is the lot of us mortals! Each of us is here for a brief sojourn; for what purpose he knows not, though he senses it. But without deeper reflections one knows from daily life that one exists for other people."
ALBERT EINSTEIN, *Physicist*

"One never really lives unless he has something to die for."
SOREN KIERKEGAARD, *Danish Philosopher*

"{Life} is a tale told by an idiot, full of sound and fury, signifying nothing."
WILLIAM SHAKESPEARE, *Macbeth*

> "The tragedy of modern man is not that he knows less and less about the meaning of his own life, but that it bothers him less and less."

VÁCLAV HAVEL, writer and former President of Czech Republic

BRIEFLY DESCRIBE THE PURPOSE OF YOUR LIFE:

_____
_____
_____
_____
_____
_____
_____
_____
_____
_____
_____
_____
_____
_____
_____
_____
_____
_____
_____

Having it All

Throughout history, we've seen people who were legendary for their ability to make money through the financial markets of the world. Some of them have become heroes and trendsetters. Here are a few examples.

JESSE LIVERMORE (1877–1940) was a legend on Wall Street. As a teenager, he gambled on stock prices and made over $1,000, which was a small fortune in the 1890s. When he took up legitimate stock trading, he lost everything in six months, but he kept going. After the market crashed in 1929, Livermore was still worth $100 million. He said, "It took me five years to learn to play the game intelligently enough to make big money when I was right." His trading techniques are still used in the market today.

Jesse Livermore deteriorated into depression over the years following the stock market crash. He was bankrupt by 1934 and killed himself in 1940. In his suicide note he told his wife he was a failure, unworthy of her love.

ARTHUR CUTTEN (1870–1936) was one of the wealthiest Americans in the 1920s. He foresaw a grain shortage coming in 1924 and by buying up grain futures, made several million dollars in eight months. He was called "the wheat king."

Arthur Cutten's speculations, along with a few others, may have led to the market crash. The U.S. government prosecuted him for fraud and tax evasion, selling his properties and taking most of his actual wealth. He died of a heart attack.

IVAR KREUGER (1880–1932) was called "the match king" for his European monopoly on the match industry. For 25 years he was a Swedish hero for the money and business he brought to his country. These individuals were among the best in the marketplace, willing to sacrifice everything to achieve worldly success. As Paul Harvey would say, "Here's the rest of the story:"

Not long after news surfaced about instability and deception in his many business holdings, Ivar Kreuger killed himself. Kreuger's companies owed more than the Swedish national debt.

CHAPTER 1 | **WHAT IS THE PURPOSE OF LIFE?**

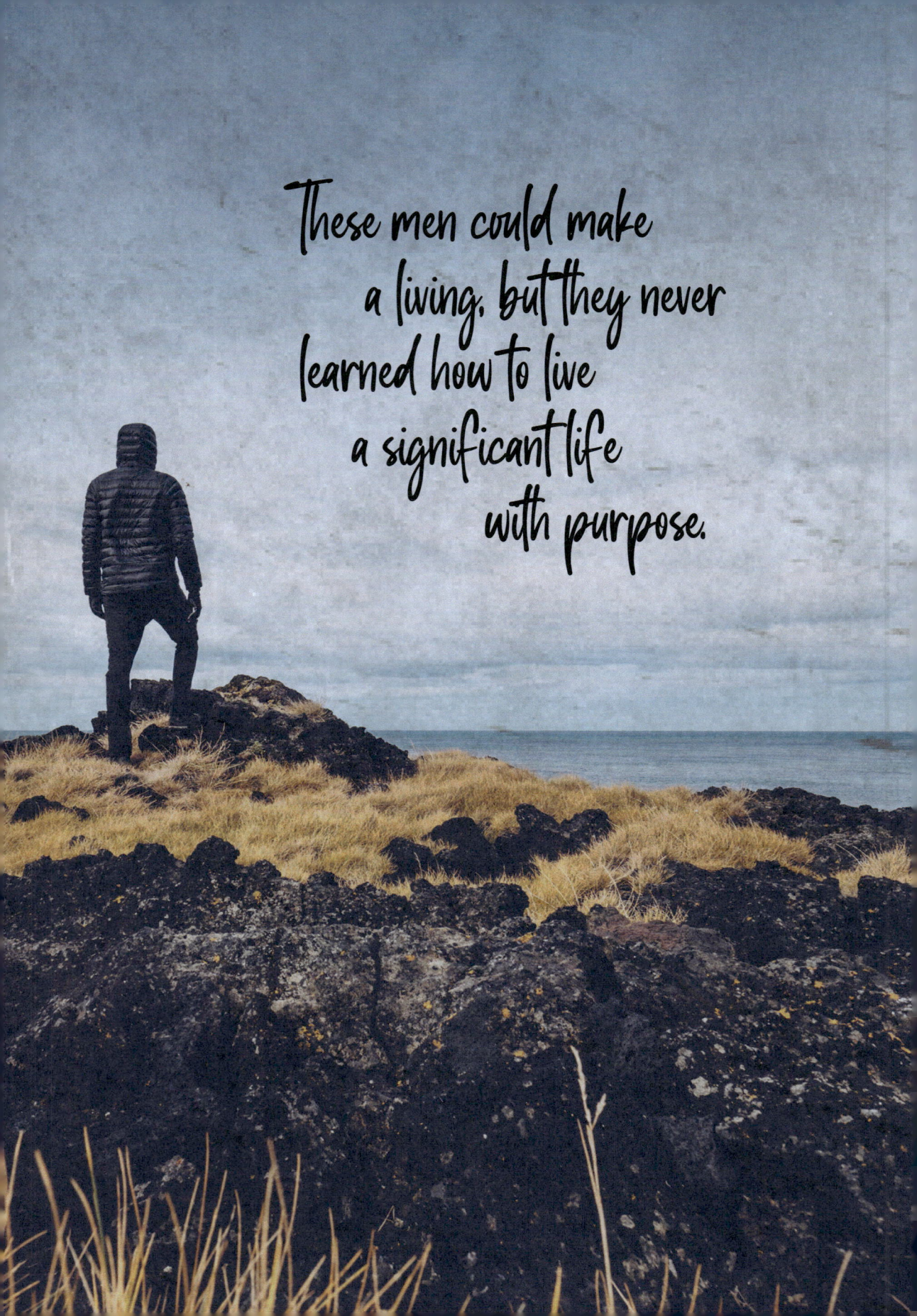

These men could make
 a living, but they never
learned how to live
 a significant life
    with purpose.

These individuals were among the best in the marketplace, willing to sacrifice everything to achieve worldly success. Like many others who make the headlines, these people could make a living, but they never learned how to live a significant life with purpose.

Reflection

HOW DO MATERIAL POSSESSIONS IMPACT A PERSON'S QUALITY OF LIFE?

_____

_____

HOW DO MATERIAL POSSESSIONS IMPACT A PERSON'S PURPOSE IN LIFE?

_____

_____

SHOULD NET WORTH, PRESTIGE, POWER, FAME, POSITION, SUCCESS AND STATUS BE CONSIDERED AS FACTORS IN DEFINING A PERSON'S SIGNIFICANCE IN LIFE? WHY OR WHY NOT?

_____

_____

We're All Wondering

All people, in all cultures, in all eras, have attempted to answer the same basic questions about life. These include:

- Who Am I?
- Why Am I Here?
- Where Did I Come From?
- Where Am I Going?

By answering these questions, we can begin to reveal our purpose in life.

CHAPTER 1 | **WHAT IS THE PURPOSE OF LIFE?**

Why Am I Here?

Recall Frank Capra's *It's a Wonderful Life* (ranked one of the top 100 movies of all time):

It is Christmas Eve, 1946. George Bailey is on the verge of suicide. With his business collapsing, he faces the scandal of bankruptcy. To top it off, he is wanted by the police for misappropriation of funds. In a desperate outburst, he declares that he wishes he'd never been born. In the midst of it all, the prayers of his family alert heaven to George's state of mind. Soon, arrangements are made to send angel Clarence Oddbody to earth to transform George's hopeless perspective.

In a strange prophetic twist, Clarence shows George what the world would have looked like if he had never been born. At first, George is unaware of the change, but as he wanders through Bedford Falls, he begins to notice subtle differences. Once a picturesque village, his hometown is now run down. The fingerprints of his life are missing from the lives of his neighbors, friends, and family. The blessings he has brought others are noticeably absent. When he encounters old friends on the street, they no longer recognize him. Even his wife reacts as if he is a stranger.

Startled by the experience, George suddenly realizes the value of his former life, even with all its flaws. He calls upon Clarence to save him. Immediately, he is transported back to normalcy. It is Christmas Day. His friends and family have organized and collected money to save George and his company from ruin. Upon seeing the lives he touched and the difference he made to the town, George Bailey concludes that he has a wonderful life after all.

> "I find it astounding that the bulk of people on out planet seem to journey through years and even decades without seriously wrestling with the fundamental question of why they are here and what they want their lives to add up to in the end. Many business and prefessional people get on a fast track in pursuit of an elisive vision of success without questioning whether they are selling themselves too cheaply by investing their precious years of life in something that, even if attained, will never satisfy."
>
> KEN BOA, *Conformed to His Image*

IT'S A WONDERFUL LIFE EXPLORES THE IMPORTANCE OF ADDING VALUE TO OTHERS. WHAT ROLE DOES THIS CONCEPT PLAY IN SHAPING YOUR PURPOSE IN LIFE?

_____

_____

_____

_____

A Study in Purpose

The 1995 movie, *Mr. Holland's Opus*, is also a study in purpose.

When Glenn Holland accepted a job as a high school music teacher, he reluctantly shelved his dream of composing an Opus, one memorable piece of music to leave his mark on the world. Instead, he found himself on a most unlikely path, pouring his life into students while learning to channel his love of music in new ways. Although the job felt like a total compromise of his calling, his passion for music never faded.

Thirty years pass and Mr. Holland learns the band and music program at his school will be canceled because of budget cuts. His life is all but spent, his Opus never written, and his school is eliminating his position. Attempts to convince the school board to reconsider are without effect. Mr. Holland decides to retire from teaching. His dreams are packed metaphorically, along with the personal items from his office.

A surprise farewell party is attended by hundreds of his former students. Now young men and women with productive lives and careers have gathered to acknowledge his impact on their lives. Topping the list is the governor of the state—also a former pupil—who addresses the gathering. Though Mr. Holland has never completed his planned masterpiece, she declares that his life work is a symphony of lives, "and we are your Opus." According to *this* definition of success, Mr. Holland's legacy is greater than he ever dreamed it could be.

CHAPTER 1 | **WHAT IS THE PURPOSE OF LIFE?**

WE ALL LEAVE SOME TYPE OF LEGACY. WHAT WOULD YOU BE REMEMBERED FOR IF YOU DIED TODAY?

_____

_____

_____

_____

What Will Your Life Add Up To?

Every person possesses gifts, talents and opportunities in this life to use as they wish. Some simply spend their lives, while others invest it in things that reflect purpose.

> "For he sees that even wise men die; the stupid and the senseless alike perish and leave their wealth to others. Their inner thought is that their houses are forever and their dwelling places to all generations; they have called their lands after their own names."
>
> **PSALMS 49:10-11**

DESCRIBE WHAT YOU WOULD REGRET LEAVING UNDONE.

_____

_____

_____

_____

Made for so Much More

We were created to need God, so how do we resolve the tension we feel apart from Him? Many religious approaches seem to emphasize a variety of tasks that need to be accomplished in order to fully qualify or justify our worthiness to God. In Ephesians 2:4-9, we see that God initiates this connection through Christ. It is described as a gift.

BOOK ONE | **LIFE QUESTIONS**

"At the close of life the question will be not, how much you have got, but how much you have given; not how much you have won, but how much you have done; not how much you have saved, but how much you have sacrificed; how much you have loved and served, not how much you were honored."

- Nathan C. Shaeffer

> "But God, being rich in mercy, because of His great love with which He loved us, even when we were dead in our transgressions, made us alive together with Christ (by grace you have been saved), and raised us up with Him, and seated us with Him in the heavenly places in Christ Jesus, so that in the ages to come He might show the surpassing riches of His grace in kindness toward us in Christ Jesus. For by grace you have been saved through faith; and that not of yourselves, it is the gift of God; not as a result of works, so that no one may boast."
>
> **EPHESIANS 2:4-9**

READ EPHESIANS 2:4-9. HOW IS GOD DESCRIBED IN THIS PASSAGE?

___

___

___

___

___

ACCORDING TO THE PASSAGE, HOW ARE WE SAVED?

___

___

___

___

___

BOOK ONE | LIFE QUESTIONS

LISTEN: *THE REASON FOR LIVING* BY TIM KELLER

LISTENING NOTES

Related Resources

- *The Purpose Driven Life: What on Earth Am I Here For?*, Rick Warren
- *Amazing Grace*, Eric Metaxas

The Take It Further section is to help you go a little deeper through challenging questions, audio recommendations, and reflective exercises. This section is optional for use in your study. You may do all, one, or none of the suggestions.

Take it Further

THINK: IF MONEY WERE NO OBJECT, WHAT LIFE DREAMS WOULD YOU PURSUE? WHY?

_____

_____

_____

_____

> "The search for the purpose of life has puzzled people for thousands of years. That's because we typically begin at the wrong starting point—ourselves. We ask self-centered questions like What do I want to be? What should I do with my life? What are my goals, my ambitions, my dreams for my future? But focusing on ourselves will never reveal our life's purpose…. Contrary to what many popular books, movies, and seminars tell you, you won't discover your life's meaning by looking within yourself…. You didn't create yourself, so there is no way you can tell yourself what you were created for!"
>
> RICK WARREN, *The Purpose Driven Life: What on Earth Am I Here For?*

OBSERVE: WATCH THE MOVIE AMAZING GRACE, WHICH IS ABOUT WILLIAM WILBERFORCE'S DEDICATION TO ABOLISH THE SLAVE TRADE IN ENGLAND DURING THE 1800S. REFLECT ON THE IMPACT ONE PERSON CAN HAVE.

_____

_____

_____

_____

CONSIDER: IN A TYPICAL WEEK, WHAT ARE THE TOP FIVE WAYS YOU SPEND YOUR TIME.

_____

_____

_____

_____

WHAT MEANING AND FULFILLMENT DO YOUR TOP FIVE BRING?

_____

_____

_____

_____

Chapter 2: Is the Bible Credible?

What do you think about the Bible? Is there anything special about it? Is it possible to make too much of it? Why do some people call it an Owner's Manual for Life, while others call it science fiction or a collection of fairy tales?

— Some Say —

"The Bible is a product of man, my dear, not of God."
SIR LEIGH TEABING, *The DaVinci Code*

"Looking for loopholes."
W. C. FIELDS, *reported reply when seen reading the Bible on his deathbed*

"No man ever believes that the Bible means what it says: He is always convinced that it says what he means."
GEORGE BERNARD SHAW, *Playwright*

WHAT QUOTABLE DESCRIPTION WOULD YOU LEAVE THE WORLD REGARDING THE BIBLE?

_____

_____

_____

WHERE DID YOU GET YOUR VIEW OF THE BIBLE? FROM YOUR UPBRINGING, A FRIEND, OR A MEMORABLE EXPERIENCE? EXPLAIN.

_____

_____

_____

A Book Like No Other

Heated debates. Denominational splits. Military crusades. And the centerpiece of all this drama? The Bible.

> "Most people are bothered by those passages in Scripture which they cannotunderstand; but as for me, I always noticed that the passages in Scripture whichtrouble me most are those which I do understand."
>
> MARK TWAIN, *author*

The last words of the Scriptures were penned almost 2000 years ago. The Bible hasn't changed since then. Neither has the controversy. In the 1300s, John Wycliffe translated the Bible from the Latin Vulgate into the English language and risked excommunication for his efforts. Two centuries later William Tyndale, a contemporary of Martin Luther, translated the New Testament directly from the Hebrew and Greek texts to produce the first genuine English translation. He was burned at the stake for his belief that the Bible was written to be accessible to everyone.

> "At least 4.9 billion people have a Bible available in their first language."
>
> WYCLIFFE.NET

Yes, the Bible deserves our attention, and our personal beliefs about this book require serious contemplation. In fact, an honest look at the Scriptures may spark an inner controversy. As you consider the questions in the following sections, two other questions may arise.

WHAT DO YOU BELIEVE ABOUT THE BIBLE?

_____

_____

_____

WHAT IMPACT WILL YOU ALLOW IT TO HAVE ON YOUR LIFE?

_____

_____

_____

> "Four out of five adults (80%) mention the Bible top-of-mind (i.e., unaided) when asked to name the books they consider to be sacred literature or holy books. This proportion is ten times more than that of the next most frequently mentioned holy book, the Koran, at 8%."
>
> AMERICAN BIBLE SOCIETY

What Is the Bible?

How do you begin to discuss a book like the Bible? Try a few vital statistics:

- It's actually a library of 66 books. These books are divided into two principle parts, the "Old Testament" (39 books) and the "New Testament" (27 books).

- Forty different writers wrote it over the course of 1500 years. These included kings, peasants, philosophers, fishermen, poets and scholars.

- The Bible was written on three different continents in three different languages.

- Despite all of the above, a consistent, complete message unfolds across its pages.

- The Bible has been read by more people and published in more languages than any other book.

CHAPTER 2 | **IS THE BIBLE CREDIBLE?**

WHICH OF THESE STATEMENTS IS MOST NOTEWORTHY TO YOU? EXPLAIN.

_____
_____
_____
_____

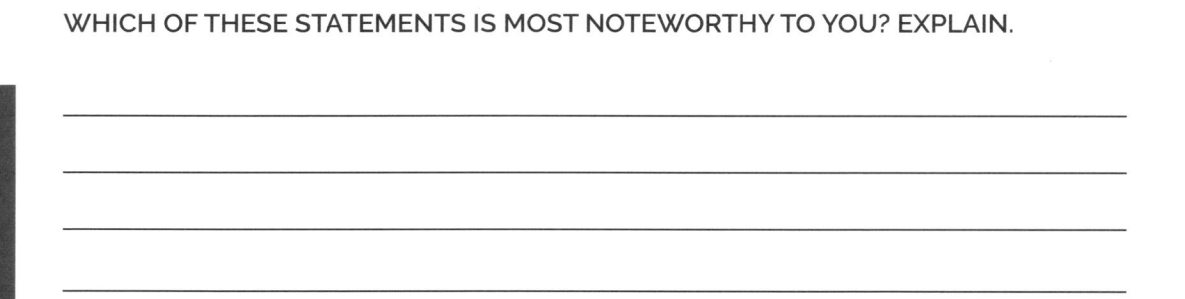

Why Was the Bible Written?

Ruth Graham once declared that she would rather spend what little time she had with her husband Billy than spend a lot of time with anyone else. As the wife of "America's Pastor," she had ample opportunity to prove that sentiment. Much of the Grahams' long, satisfying marriage was spent apart, without the connection afforded by today's technology. During those years when their children were small and Billy's travels kept him away for months at a time, they wrote letters. Lots of them.

In 1955, Billy wrote to Ruth from Glasgow:

> "I don't have to tell you that you are in my mind every moment and that I love you with all my heart, and miss you so much that it hurts… Naturally, I think of you a thousand times a day and each little experience I wish I could share with you."

Billy Graham's letters reveal a surprising vulnerability in the very public man. He wrote, not only to keep his wife informed, but also to solicit her help. He expressed the tenderness between them. Ruth, onthe other hand, often wrote to lighten Billy's load with humor and truth. She reserved her loneliness for her prayer journal. The sum of their letters reflect a growing intimacy and devotion that flourished despite—perhaps because of—their many separations.

Could the Bible be meant to connect us intimately and personally to God? That would make it far more than a theological treatise, wouldn't it? Instead of a document designed to fill us with knowledge, the Scriptures would be a divine love letter to us.

"Your letters have given me inspiration, quieted my nerves. They bring me so close to you."

Billy to Ruth, *Glasgow, 1955.*

Three Purposes for the Bible

1. TO REVEAL GOD TO PEOPLE

The Bible gives finite people a way of knowing something about an infinite God.

> "And the Word became flesh, and dwelt among us, and we saw His glory, glory as of the only begotten from the Father, full of grace and truth."
> **JOHN 1:14**

> "He who has My commandments and keeps them is the one who loves Me; and he who loves Me will be loved by My Father, and I will love him and will disclose Myself to him."
> **JOHN 14:21**

GOD USES THE BIBLE TO REVEAL HIMSELF. HOW DOES THIS AFFECT THE WAY YOU THINK ABOUT IT OR USE IT?

_____
_____
_____
_____

2. TO REVEAL TO PEOPLE HOW TO LIVE

> "So keep and do them, for that is your wisdom and your understanding in the sight of the peoples who will hear all these statutes and say, 'Surely this great nation is a wise and understanding people.'"
> **DEUTERONOMY 4:6**

> "This book of the law shall not depart from your mouth, but you shall "This book of the law shall not depart from your mouth, but you shall meditate on it day and night, so that you may be careful to do according to all that is written in it; for then you will make your way prosperous, and then you will have success.
> **JOSHUA 1:8**

DOES THE BIBLE STRIKE YOU AS PRACTICAL AND RELEVANT FOR LIFE IN TODAY'S WORLD? WHY OR WHY NOT?

_____

_____

_____

> Today, we possess over 5,600 ancient Greek manuscripts for the New Testament, and 19,000 copies in other ancient languages. Latin and Coptic copies go back to the 2nd century. We even have a papyrus fragment of *The Gospel of John* from 29 years after it was first written. Complete volumes of the New Testament date to the 4th century A.D.
>
> Compare this with the second best-preserved literary work of antiquity, Homer's *Iliad*, which has only 643 preserved manuscripts. The *Iliad* is believed to have been written in the 8th century B.C.
>
> adapted from *Evidence that Demands a Verdict*, JOSH MCDOWELL

3. TO REVEAL HOW GOD INTERACTS WITH PEOPLE THROUGH TIME

> "God, who at various times and in various ways spoke in time past to the fathers by the prophets.'"
> **HEBREWS 1:1**

> "For whatever was written in earlier times was written for our instruction, so that through perseverance and the encouragement of the Scriptures we might have hope."
> **ROMANS 15:4**

CHAPTER 2 | **IS THE BIBLE CREDIBLE?**

WHAT DO GOD'S INTERACTIONS WITH ANCIENT PEOPLE SUGGEST ABOUT HIS NATURE? IS THIS INFORMATION USEFUL TO DAY? WHY OR WHY NOT?

_____

_____

_____

Is the Bible Credible?

Passing It On

It's easy to forget that the Bible predates the printing press by over a thousand years. To preserve it, the words were copied laboriously on papyrus. Very few people ever saw a manuscript. That privilege was reserved for religious officials. Over centuries, the Jews nurtured and preserved the writings, carefully recopying each letter. They adhered to strict guidelines. If a single letter or syllable was wrong, the entire copy was destroyed and the process was started over. The early Christians continued the practice of precision, passing along the written Word carefully from generation to generation.

Archaeological Findings

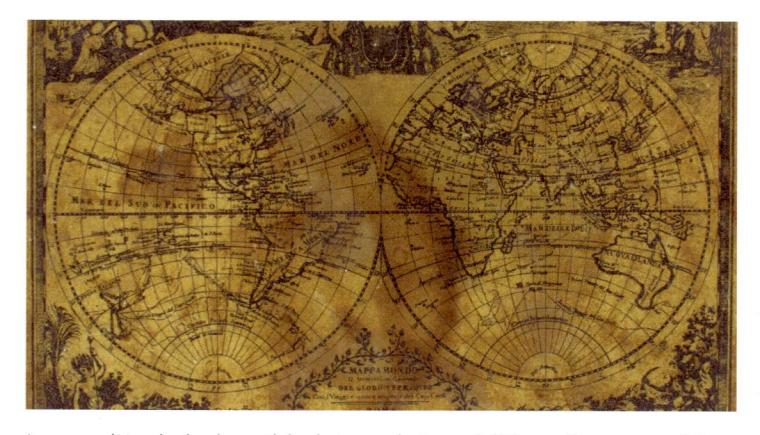

"Probably the Dead Sea Scrolls have had the greatest Biblical impact. They have provided Old Testament manuscripts approximately 1,000 years older than our previous oldest manuscript. The Dead Sea Scrolls have demonstrated that the Old Testament was accurately transmitted during this interval. In addition, they provide a wealth of information on the times leading up to, and during, the life of Christ." *(Dr. Bryant Wood, Archaeologist)*

> "Approximately 2,500 prophecies appear in the pages of the Bible, about 2,000 of which already have been fulfilled to the letter—no errors. Since the probability for any one of these prophecies having been fulfilled by chance averages less than one in ten, and since the prophecies are for the most part independent of one another, the odds for all these prophecies having been fulfilled by chance without error is less than one in 10^{2000}!"
>
> HUGH ROSS, ASTROPHYSICIST, WWW.REASONS.ORG

Fulfilled Prophecy

Fulfilled prophecies also validate the authenticity of the Bible's contents—including Jesus' claim to be the Son of God. There is an amazing consistency between the prophecies which preceded Jesus by hundreds of years and His fulfillment of those ancient words. In Ted J. Brasier's book, *Get the Point: Plotting the Way Back to Life*, he gives the following illustration:

> "Suppose that we take 10^{17} silver dollars and lay them on the face of Texas. They'll cover all of the state two feet deep. Now mark one of these silver dollars and stir the whole mass thoroughly, all over the state. Blindfold a man and tell him that he can travel as far as he wishes, but he must pick up one silver dollar and say that this is the right one. What chance would he have of getting the right one? Just the same chance that the prophets would've had of writing these eight prophecies and having them all come true in any one man, from their day to the present time, providing they wrote them in their own wisdom."

The predictions and the features of Christ's life correspond in astonishing detail. The chart on the next page briefly lists some of the prophecies made concerning the Christ and how Jesus fulfilled them.

CHAPTER 2 | IS THE BIBLE CREDIBLE?

TOPIC	PROPHECY	FULFILLMENT
BIRTHPLACE	"As for you, Bethlehem Ephrathah, too little to be among the clans of Judah, from you One will go forth for Me to be ruler in Israel. His goings forth are from long ago, from the days of eternity." *Micah 5:2 (700 BC)*	"Jesus was born in Bethlehem in Judea." *Matthew 2:1*
BORN OF A VIRGIN	"Therefore the Lord Himself will give you a sign: Behold, a virgin will be with child and bear a son, and she will call His name Immanuel." *Isaiah 7:14 (700 BC)*	"His mother Mary had been betrothed to Joseph, before they came together she was found to be with child by the Holy Spirit." *Matthew 1:18*
HIS TRIUMPHAL ENTRY	"Rejoice greatly, O daughter of Zion! Shout in triumph, O daughter of Jerusalem! Behold, your king is coming to you; He is just and endowed with salvation, humble, and mounted on a donkey, even on a colt, the foal of a donkey." *Zechariah 9:9 (500 BC)*	"[The crowd] took the branches of the palm trees and went out to meet Him and began to shout, 'Hosanna! Blessed is he who comes in the name of the Lord, even the King of Israel.' Jesus, finding a young donkey, sat on it." *John 12:13-14*
BETRAYED BY A FRIEND	"Even my close friend in whom I trusted, who ate my bread, has lifted up his heel against me." *Psalms 41:9 (1000 BC)*	"Then Judas Iscariot, who was one of the twelve, went off to the chief priests in order to betray Him to them. *Mark 14:10*
HIS REJECTION	"He was despised and forsaken of men, a man of sorrows and acquainted with grief; and like one from whom men hide their face He was despised, and we did not esteem Him." *Isaiah 53:3 (700 BC)*	"He came to His own, and those who were His own did not receive Him." *John 1:11*
CRUCIFIED WITH SINNERS	"Therefore I will give him a portion among the great, and he will divide the spoils with the strong, because he poured out his life unto death, and was numbered with the transgressors. For he bore the sin of many, and made intercession for the transgressors." *Isaiah 53:12*	"At that time two robbers were crucified with Him, one on the right and one on the left." *Matthew 27:38*
HANDS AND FEET PIERCED	"They have pierced my hands and my feet." *Psalms 22:16 (1000 BC)*	"Put your finger here; see my hands. Reach out your hand and put it into my side. Stop doubting and believe." *John 20:27*
HIS RESURRECTION	"For You will not abandon my soul to Sheol; nor will You allow Your Holy One to undergo decay." *Psalms 16:10 (1000 BC)*	"[You] put to death the Prince of life, the one whom God raised from the dead," *Acts 3:15*
HIS ASCENSION	"You ascended on High." *Psalms 68:18 (1000 BC)*	"He was lifted up while they were looking on, and a cloud received Him out of their sight." *Acts 1:9*

What Does the Bible Say about Itself?

Let's say you've written an email to one of your top employees. The sole purpose of your message is to commend a job well done on a recent project. You're not only grateful for this man's performance, you know the value of good people and you're making sure you accurately express your thoughts. You copy a draft to a co-worker before sending it.

Imagine your surprise when your esteemed employee tenders his resignation that afternoon. You mention the glowing email in your draft box. "Oh, I know about that," replies the employee, "I heard you were about to fire me, so I decided to save you the trouble." Somehow your words were misrepresented and a completely erroneous message was passed along. Your words were not allowed to speak for themselves —with disastrous results.

If God has spoken, shouldn't we let His words speak for themselves? In addition to the abundance of commentaries about the Bible, the Bible makes some important statements about itself. Consider what the apostle Paul wrote to his protégé Timothy about the Holy Scriptures:

> "You, however, continue in the things you have learned and become convinced of, knowing from whom you have learned them, and that from childhood you have known the sacred writings which are able to give you the wisdom that leads to salvation through faith which is in Christ Jesus. All Scripture is inspired by God and profitable for teaching, for reproof, for correction, for training in righteousness; so that the man of God may be adequate, equipped for every good work."
>
> **2 Timothy 3:14-17**

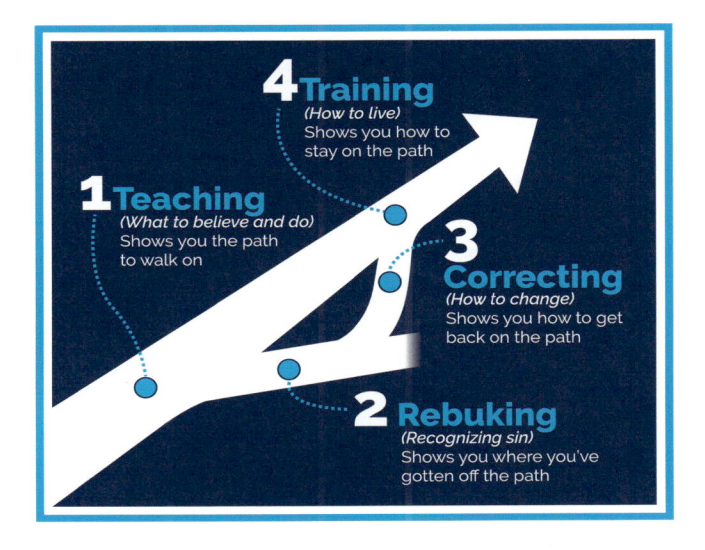

4 Training (How to live) — Shows you how to stay on the path

1 Teaching (What to believe and do) — Shows you the path to walk on

3 Correcting (How to change) — Shows you how to get back on the path

2 Rebuking (Recognizing sin) — Shows you where you've gotten off the path

CHAPTER 2 | **IS THE BIBLE CREDIBLE?** 25

WHAT ARE THE IMPLICATIONS OF PAUL'S CLAIM THAT THE BIBLE'S CONTENTS ARE INSPIRED BY GOD?

_____
_____
_____

HOW WOULD YOU DESCRIBE THE BIBLE IN RESPONSE TO THIS CHAPTER?

_____
_____
_____

In the Old Testament alone, the writers claim to be writing or speaking God's words over 2,600 times. In the New Testament, the Apostle Peter refers to these men:

> "So we have the prophetic word made more sure, to which you do well to pay attention as to a lamp shining in a dark place, until the day dawns and the morning star arises in your hearts. But know this first of all, that no prophecy of Scripture is a matter of one's own interpretation, for no prophecy was ever made by an act of human will, but men moved by the Holy Spirit spoke from God."
> **2 PETER 1:19-21**

ACCORDING TO THESE VERSES, WHERE DID THE PROPHECY ORIGINATE?

_____
_____
_____

HOW HAS THIS CHAPTER AFFECTED YOUR VIEW OF THE BIBLE?

_____
_____
_____

WHAT QUESTIONS OR CONCERNS DO YOU STILL HAVE ABOUT THE CREDIBILITY OF THE BIBLE?

___

LISTEN: *IS THE BIBLE REALLY TRUSTWORTHY* BY KEN BOA

LISTENING NOTES

___

Related Resources

- *The New Evidence that Demands a Verdict,* Josh McDowell
- www.jcstudies.com
- *"How Can the Bible be Authoritative?"* by N.T. Wright

The Take It Further section is to help you go a little deeper through challenging questions, audio recommendations, and reflective exercises. This section is optional for use in your study. You may do all, one, or none of the suggestions.

Take it Further

THINK: HOW WOULD YOU ANSWER SOMEONE WHO SAYS THE BIBLE IS NOT RELIABLE?

_____
_____
_____
_____
_____

CONSIDER: LISTEN TO *A CELEBRATION* BY IRISH ROCK BAND U2. IS THERE A MESSAGE ABOUT THE TRUTH OF THE BIBLE IN THE WORDS OF THIS SONG?

_____
_____
_____
_____
_____

Notes

Chapter 3: Where is God?

If God is there, where is He when I really need Him? I have questions and struggles and needs, and I'm not sure He even knows about them. Is He relevant to my daily life? Does He even care?

— Some Say —

"If someone were to prove to me right this minute that God, in all his luminousness, exists, it wouldn't change a single aspect of my behavior."
LUIS BUÑUEL, *Spanish filmmaker*

" One must keep pointing out that Christianity is a statement which, if false, is of no importance, and, if true, is of infinite importance. The one thing it cannot be is moderately important."
C. S. LEWIS, *professor and author*

"The trouble with many people today is that they haven't found a God big enough for modern needs."
J. B. PHILLIPS, *English theologian*

"To you, I'm an atheist; to God, I'm the loyal Opposition."
WOODY ALLEN, *actor*

WHAT THOUGHTS ABOUT GOD ARE FOREMOST IN YOUR MIND?

_____

_____

_____

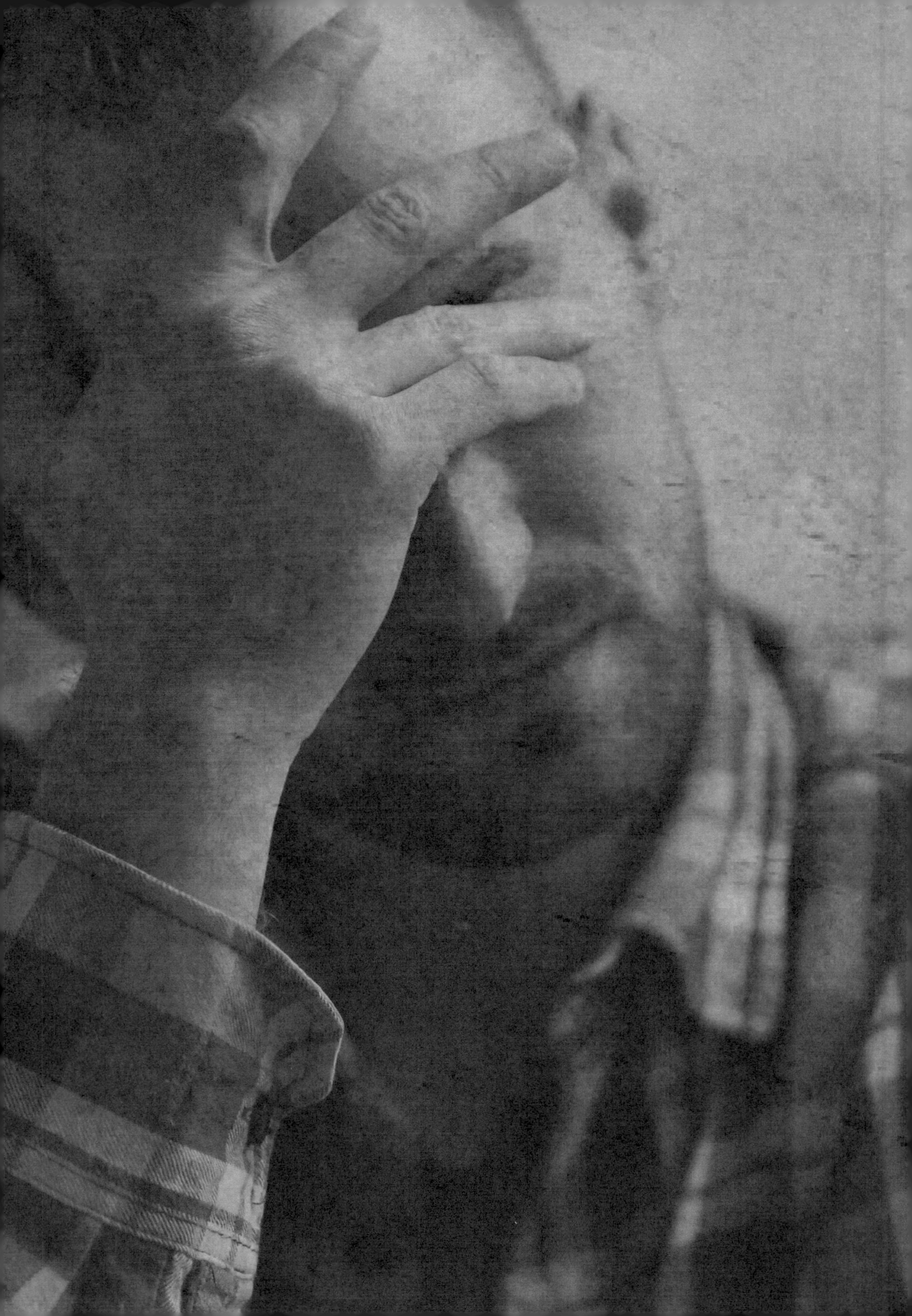

Is God Relevant?

In his book *The Portable Atheist*, Christopher Hitchens makes a distinction between the existence of God and the existence of an intervening God. As an articulate representative of atheism today, Mr. Hitchens points out that his dispute is primarily with the latter. He recognizes that any belief system regarding a god presumes that God's "wishes have been made known or can be determined."

This, then, is the hinge of all human thought about God: not Does He exist?, but Is He relevant? Christians affirm God's relevance in their lives, but what about our day-to-day experience? What about real life? Where is God? What do we do with the confusion we often feel about Him? We look at someone we love who is suffering and find it impossible not to ask, "God, where are you?" We're, at best, confused and, at worst, cynical.

But we just discovered God's desire to reveal Himself in His Word. We know He has something to say, that He is relevant. So, what does that look like?

CONSIDER THESE STEREOTYPICAL VIEWS OF GOD

- **COSMIC KILLJOY** - God limits me and doesn't let me have fun.
- **DOTING GRANDFATHER** - God gives me unconcerned pats on the head when I do something wrong.
- **MAGIC GENIE** - God grants every request that seems reasonable.
- **ANGRY JUDGE** - God stands ready to punish me whenever I mess up.

HOW WOULD YOU DESCRIBE GOD?

_____

_____

_____

THE TRUTH

- God's limits are for our protection.
- God takes great offense to sin and disobedience.

CHAPTER 3 | **WHERE IS GOD?**

- God knows what is best and may withhold wisely because of His full knowledge and greater purposes.
- God is holy and just, but He is also a loving, forgiving Father.

TO WHAT EXTENT WOULD YOU SAY HE IS INVOLVED IN YOUR PERSONAL LIFE AND CONCERNS?

_____
_____
_____

TAKE INVENTORY

From the list below, which areas to do currently find to be a challenge?

- [ ] Relationships
- [ ] Job
- [ ] Marriage
- [ ] Finances
- [ ] Kids
- [ ] Family
- [ ] Education
- [ ] Other

WHY ARE THESE CHALLENGING?

_____
_____
_____

Food for Thought

Gallup and other polls indicate that 90% of Americans believe in a "higher power." At the same time, pollsters tell us that a decreasing number of people consider God when they face life's challenges.

HOW DO YOU ACCOUNT FOR THIS DISCREPANCY?

_____
_____

Does God Know Me?

Regardless of whether a person thinks God is relevant, God is all-powerful and all-knowing. Complete these sentences:

IF GOD KNOWS ME COMPLETLY, IT'S A LITTLE SCARY BECAUSE:

_____

_____

_____

IF GOD KNOWS ME COMPLETLY, IT'S ENCOURAGING BECAUSE:

_____

_____

_____

God Knows Your Struggles

> "No matter how successful we become ... questions always lurk in the shadows, just waiting to pounce on us when life's inevitable problems overtake us. We strain to keep it all together, but the pressure is often like a tight band around our chest. Sometimes, the gravity of our debts and duties weighs us down so much that our interior posture is in a slump— even if we fake it and stand tall to the world."
>
> PAT MORLEY, *Man in the Mirror*

In the question of God's relevance, let's examine life in the context of work, relationships, money and crisis.

DOES MORLEY'S WORD PICTURE DESCRIBE YOU AT ALL? EXPLAIN.

_____

_____

CHAPTER 3 | **WHERE IS GOD?**

God and Work

Colossians 3:23-25 instructs workers in the following way: "Whatever you do, do your work heartily, as for the Lord rather than for men, knowing that from the Lord you will receive the reward of the inheritance. It is the Lord Christ whom you serve. For he who does wrong will receive the consequences of the wrong which he has done, and that without partiality."

> "If it falls to your lot to be a street sweeper, sweep the streets like Michelangelo painted pictures, like Shakespeare wrote poetry, like Beethoven composed music; sweep streets so well that all the host of Heaven and earth will have to pause and say, "Here lived a great street sweeper, who swept his job well."
>
> — MARTIN LUTHER KING, JR.

IN YOUR OWN WORDS, WHAT ARE THE PRINCIPLES GOD GIVES ABOUT WORK IN *COLOSSIANS 3:23-25*?

_____
_____
_____

HOW WOULD THE WORLD CHANGE IF PEOPLE FOLLOWED THESE PRINCIPLES?

_____
_____
_____

IN WHAT SPECIFIC WAYS WOULD YOUR DAILY LIFE CHANGE IF YOU FOLLOWED THE STANDARD DESCRIBED IN THE PASSAGE?

_____

_____

_____

God and Relationships

Think about your significant relationships and list the five people most important to you:

1. _____

2. _____

3. _____

4. _____

5. _____

> "Love is patient, love is kind and is not jealous; love does not brag and is not arrogant, does not act unbecomingly; it does not seek its own, is not provoked, does not take into account a wrong suffered, does not rejoice in unrighteousness, but rejoices with the truth; bears all things, believes all things, hopes all things, endures all things."
>
> **1 CORINTHIANS 13:4-7**

HOW DOES THE QUALITY OF YOUR SIGNIFICANT RELATIONSHIPS COMPARE TO THIS DESCRIPTION?

_____

_____

_____

CHAPTER 3 | **WHERE IS GOD?**

"Love is patient, love is kind and is not jealous; love does not brag and is not arrogant, does not act unbecomingly; it does not seek its own, is not provoked, does not take into account a wrong suffered, does not rejoice in unrighteousness, but rejoices with the truth; bears all things, believes all things, hopes all things, endures all things." 1 Corinthians 13:4-7

WHICH ATTITUDES DESCRIBED PRESENT THE GREATEST CHALLENGE TO YOU?

_____

_____

_____

> Husbands, love your wives, just as Christ loved the church
> and gave himself up for her.
> **EPHESIANS 5:25**

HAVE HAVE YOU EVER SEEN A MARRIAGE THAT FITS THE DESCRIPTION FOUND IN EPHESIANS 5:25? DESCRIBE THAT RELATIONSHIP:

_____

_____

_____

> "The Bible can be described in one word – relationships."
> KEN BOA

WHAT PRIMARY THEME(S) EMERGE FROM GOD'S ATTITUDE TOWARD RELATIONSHIPS AS REVEALED IN SCRIPTURE?

_____

_____

_____

CHAPTER 3 | **WHERE IS GOD?**

God and Money

This combination conjures up visions of televangelists' indiscretions or the discomfort of sitting through a sermon on tithing. It's fodder for late-night comedy on TV and caricature in Southern novels.

We don't like to talk about God and money. In fact, many would consider it seriously inappropriate as subject matter for polite conversation. Does that mean we should neglect the matter altogether? Would God prefer for us to "be nice" and never mention it?

You might be surprised to learn that the Bible has more to say about money than any other single subject—over 2,300 verses make reference to it. Why? It has been said that our handling of finances conveys more about us—and our values—than anything else. Money is complicated today. So how could an ancient book like the Bible possibly advise us on money management? Is it relevant?

A few mentions of money in the Bible:

> "The rich rules over the poor, and the borrower becomes the lender's slave."
> **PROVERBS 22:7**
>
> "For we have brought nothing into this world, so we cannot take anything out of it, either."
> **1 TIMOTHY 6:7**
>
> "He who loves money will not be satisfied with money, nor he who loves abundance with its income. This too is vanity."
> **ECCLESIASTES 5:10**
>
> "For where your treasure is, there your heart will be also."
> **MATTHEW 6:21**

CAN YOU GIVE EXAMPLES OF THESE PRINCIPLES IN ACTION TODAY?

_____
_____
_____

WHICH OF THESE LIFE ISSUES – WORK, RELATIONSHIPS, OR MONEY – PRESENT THE GREATEST CONCERNS TO YOU? EXPLAIN.

_____
_____
_____

God and Crisis Management

People tend to say, I'm thinking about you, when they don't know what else to say—when our struggles either embarrass or concern them. It's comforting to know someone is thinking of us, but it only goes so far to ease our pain, doesn't it? Is this all the Bible has to say when we hurt? Are God's words impotent when our hearts are injured and in danger of breaking? Perhaps there is truth, but is there relief? There may be answers, but are those truths satisfying? If God is thinking of us, what are His thoughts?

> "These things I have spoken to you, so that in Me you may have peace. In the world you have tribulation, but take courage; I have overcome the world."
> **JOHN 16:33**
>
> "Be anxious for nothing, but in everything by prayer and supplication with thanksgiving let your requests be made known to God. And the peace of God, which surpasses all comprehension, will guard your hearts and your minds in Christ Jesus."
> **PHILIPPIANS 4:6-7**

CHAPTER 3 | **WHERE IS GOD?**

HAVE YOU EVER SENSED GOD'S PERSONAL CONCERN FOR YOU IN THESE TYPES OF STRUGGLES? DISCUSS.

_____
_____
_____

Can God Be Trusted?

Life teaches us to be skeptical. Everywhere we turn it seems someone is out to take advantage of us. There's no end to the list of people who might hurt and disappoint us: spam solicitations, telemarketers, opportunistic co-workers, deceitful business partners and selfish relatives.

HOW DOES OUR SKEPTICISM TOWARD PEOPLE INFLUENCE OUR ABILITY TO TRUST GOD? EXPLAIN.

_____
_____
_____

While people may change their opinions and loyalties, God will never fail you.

> "For He Himself has said, 'I will never desert you, nor will I ever forsake you,' ... Jesus Christ is the same yesterday and today and forever."
>
> **HEBREWS 13:5B, 8**

BOOK ONE | LIFE QUESTIONS

WHAT DOES THIS PASSAGE REVEAL ABOUT GOD'S CHARACTER?

_____
_____
_____

Read **DEUTERONOMY 31:6-9:**

"Be strong and courageous, do not be afraid or tremble at them, for the Lord your God is the one who goes with you. He will not fail you or forsake you. Then Moses called to Joshua and said to him in the sight of all Israel, 'Be strong and courageous, for you shall go with this people into the land which the Lord has sworn to their fathers to give them, and you shall give it to them as an inheritance. The Lord is the one who goes ahead of you; He will be with you. He will not fail you or forsake you. Do not fear or be dismayed."

WHAT DOES THIS PASSAGE SAY MY RESPONSE SHOULD BE?

_____
_____
_____
_____

What Does God Care About?

Regardless of how much you know about God, He knows you intimately.

> "O LORD, You have searched me and known me. You know when I sit down and when I rise up; you understand my thought from afar you scrutinize my path and my lying down, and are intimately acquainted with all my ways. Even before there is a word on my tongue, behold, O LORD, You know it all. You have enclosed me behind and before, and laid Your hand upon me. Such knowledge is too wonderful for me; it is too high, I cannot attain to it. Where can I go from Your Spirit? Or where can I flee from Your presence? If I ascend to heaven, You are there."
>
> **PSALM 139:1-8A**

CHAPTER 3 | **WHERE IS GOD?**

ACCORDING TO THE PASSAGE, HOW MUCH IS GOD INVOLVED WITH US?

_____
_____
_____

IN WHAT SPECIFIC WAYS IS GOD INVOLVED PERSONALLY IN EVERYDAY LIFE?

_____
_____
_____

> "For this reason I say to you, do not be worried about your life, as to what you will eat or what you will drink; nor for your body, as to what you will put on. Is not life more than food, and the body more than clothing? Look at the birds of the air, that they do not sow, nor reap nor gather into barns, and yet your heavenly Father feeds them. Are you not worth much more than they? And who of you by being worried can add a single hour to his life? And why are you worried about clothing? Observe how the lilies of the field grow; they do not toil nor do they spin, yet I say to you that not even Solomon in all his glory clothed himself like one of these. But if God so clothes the grass of the field, which is alive today and tomorrow is thrown into the furnace, will He not much more clothe you? You of little faith! Do not worry then, saying, 'What will we eat?' or 'What will we drink?' or 'What will we wear for clothing?' For the Gentiles eagerly seek all these things; for your heavenly Father knows that you need all these things. But seek first His kingdom and His righteousness, and all these things will be added to you. So do not worry about tomorrow; for tomorrow will care for itself. Each day has enough trouble of its own."
>
> **MATTHEW 6:25-34**

Since God cares enough about us to provide instruction for us regarding work, relationships, money and crises, He is relevant to life.

WHAT PROMISES DOES GOD MAKE? HOW ARE THESE PROMISES RELEVANT TO YOUR LIFE?

_____
_____
_____

LISTEN: *IT'S NOT AS BAD AS YOU THINK* BY PHILIP DE COURCY

LISTENING NOTES

_____
_____
_____
_____
_____

Related Resources

- *Man in the Mirror*, Pat Morley
- *Disappointment with God*, Philip Yancey
- *The One Year Book of Hope*, Nancy Gutherie

CHAPTER 3 | **WHERE IS GOD?**

> *The Take It Further section is to help you go a little deeper through challenging questions, audio recommendations, and reflective exercises. This section is optional for use in your study. You may do all, one, or none of the suggestions.*

Take it Further

THINK: IF GOD CARES SO MUCH, WHY IS LIFE SO HARD AT TIMES?

_____
_____
_____
_____
_____
_____
_____

CONSIDER: WHICH OF THE ISSUES DISCUSSED IN THIS SESSION CAUSE YOU THE MOST DIFFICULTY? WHAT DO YOU WISH GOD WOULD DO TO HELP YOU?

_____
_____
_____
_____
_____

LISTEN TO *IN GOD WE TRUST* BY RACHEL LAMPA. HOW COULD THE LYRICS OF THIS SONG APPLY TO YOU?

_____
_____
_____
_____

Chapter 4: Who is Jesus?

If you want to create an awkward silence at a business lunch or dinner party, ask the question, Who is Jesus? Mention God and you're within most social boundaries. But, Jesus, He provokes intense reactions. What is it about God's Son that triggers that kind of response? Could it be that Jesus causes people to examine their lives with more honesty? If Jesus is the flashpoint, does that mean our feelings about Him must be examined as well? Are we free to be bored with Him or to embrace faith in Him disinterestedly?

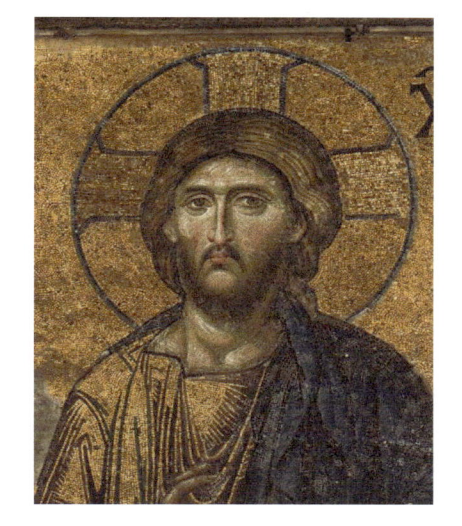

What do we label a person who is so bound to strict religiosity they can't see past their rules? Someone so enamored with their own picture of how things are supposed to be they can't entertain different options. A close-minded person? A legalist? We call such people Pharisees.

The Pharisees began as the elite, the respected leaders of their day. Today the term Pharisee is instantly understood as a parody of righteousness. A caricature of uppity religion.

For two millennia the designation has served as a byword for spiritual blindness. But in the beginning they were the insiders. If God were to show up, surely they would be the first to recognize Him.

But they didn't.

The Pharisees—who had memorized Scripture—not only missed the truth about Jesus, they rallied their entire political machinery against Him. Here's why: He didn't fit their preconceived notions. Everything they assumed the Messiah would be, Jesus was not.

And that's the danger we face today. Our ideas about Jesus get in the way of our understanding of Him. The challenge is to allow Jesus to speak for Himself, to define Himself, instead of seeking to confirm or refute our concept of Him.

> "As the centuries pass, the evidence is accumulating that, measured by His effect on history, Jesus is the most influential life ever lived on this planet."
> KENNETH SCOTT LATOURETTE, *historian*

Some Say

"I am an historian, I am not a believer, but I must confess as an historian that this penniless preacher from Nazareth is irrevocably the very center of history. Jesus Christ is easily the most dominant figure in all history."
H.G. WELLS, *British author*

"As a child I received instruction both in the Bible and in the Talmud. I am a Jew, but I am enthralled by the luminous figure of the Nazarene ... No one can read the Gospels without feeling the actual presence of Jesus. His personality pulsates in every word. No myth is filled with such life."
ALBERT EINSTEIN, *mathematician*

"I know men, and I tell you, Jesus Christ was no mere man ... Alexander, Caesar, Charlemagne, and myself founded empires; but on what did we rest the creations of our genius? Upon force. Jesus Christ alone founded his empire upon love; and, at this hour, millions of men would die for him."
NAPOLEON, *at his defeat at Waterloo*

"The day will come when the mystical generation of Jesus by the Supreme Being in the womb of a virgin will be classed with the fable of the generation of Minerva in the brain of Jupiter."
THOMAS JEFFERSON, *in a letter to John Adams, April 11, 1823*

"A man who was merely a man and said the sort of things Jesus said would not be a great moral teacher. He would either be a lunatic—on the level with a man who says he is a poached egg—or he would be the devil of hell. You must take your choice. Either this was, and is, the Son of God, or else a madman or something worse. You can shut him up for a fool or you can fall at his feet and call him Lord and God. But let us not come with any patronizing nonsense about his being a great human teacher. He has not left that open to us."
C.S. LEWIS, *Mere Christianity*

WHICH OF THESE THOUGHTS CAPTURES YOUR PERCEPTIONS OF JESUS?

_____
_____
_____

Do You Believe Jesus Existed?

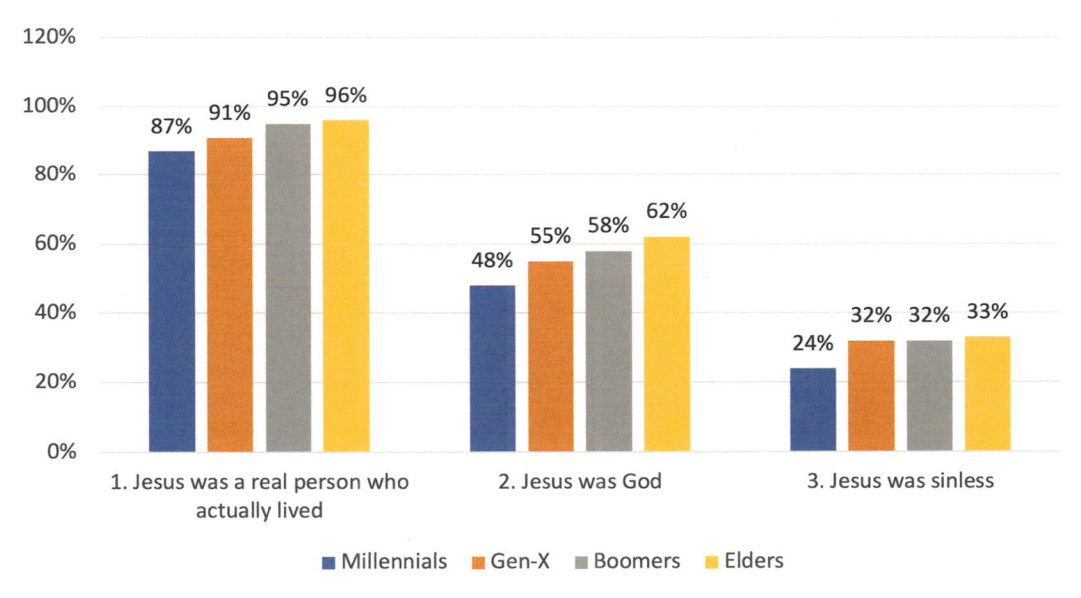

	Millennials	Gen-X	Boomers	Elders
1. Jesus was a real person who actually lived	87%	91%	95%	96%
2. Jesus was God	48%	55%	58%	62%
3. Jesus was sinless	24%	32%	32%	33%

(Credit: Barna, What do Americans Believe About Jesus (2015))

WHICH POINT OF VIEW ABOVE MATCHES YOURS? EXPLAIN.

_____
_____
_____

CHAPTER 4 | **WHO IS JESUS?**

> "Scholars today who treat the gospels as credible historical documents do so in the full light of the [stringent analytical study for the past 200 years], not by closing their minds to it. A problem arises in this television age from the exposure of the public to a bewildering variety of opinions about the gospels in particular and the New Testament in general, including both the current scholarly consensus (if such a thing exists today) and every sort of way-out interpretation of the data, with little or no guidance being given about the criteria by which competing views are to be assessed and a reasonable conclusion reached."
>
> F.F. BRUCE, FORWARD TO *THE HISTORICAL RELIABILITY OF THE GOSPELS*, BY CRAIG BLOMBERG

IN YOUR OPINION, WHO IS THE MOST INFLUENTIAL PERSON ALIVE TODAY?

WHO WAS THE MOST INFLUENTIAL PERSON OF THE LAST 100 YEARS?

THE MOST INFLUENTIAL IN ALL OF HUMAN HISTORY?

A number of historians would say that Jesus, who lived for about 30 years, lived a simple life, had no political power and never traveled extensively, has had the most profound influence on our world.

WHAT WOULD YOU SAY ABOUT JESUS?

Jesus' Humanity

> What did Jesus claim about Himself? Jesus claimed to be both fully human and fully God.

Did Jesus experience normal human feelings? What about boredom or confusion? What about temptation, even lust? Did he grow weary? Get hungry?

The Bible describes Jesus in physical and emotional terms:

- "And Jesus kept increasing in wisdom and stature, and in favor with God and men." **LUKE 2:52**

- "Now in the morning, when He was returning to the city, He became hungry." **MATTHEW 21:18**

- "... Jacob's well was there. So Jesus, being wearied from His journey, was sitting thus by the well. It was about the sixth hour." **JOHN 4:6**

- "Therefore, since the children share in flesh and blood, He Himself likewise also partook of the same, that through death He might render powerless him who had the power of death, that is, the devil." **HEBREWS 2:14**

- "Therefore, He had to be made like His brethren in all things, so that He might become a merciful and faithful high priest in things pertaining to God, to make propitiation for the sins of the people. For since He Himself was tempted in that which He has suffered, He is able to come to the aid of those who are tempted." **HEBREWS 2:17-18**

- "Jesus wept." **JOHN 11:35**

WHAT DO THESE VERSES SAY TO YOU ABOUT HIS HUMANITY?

___

SO WAS JESUS HUMAN? WHAT DOES THAT MEAN TO THE HUMAN RACE? TO INDIVIDUAL HUMANS?

___

> "Therefore, since we have a great high priest who has passed through the heavens, Jesus the Son of God, let us hold fast our confession. For we do not have a high priest who cannot sympathize with our weaknesses, but One who has been tempted in all things as we are, yet without sin."
> **HEBREWS 4:14-15**

ACCORDING TO THIS PASSAGE, WHAT DID JESUS SHARE IN COMMON WITH US?

___

IN WHAT PRIMARY WAY WAS HE DIFFERENT?

___

BOOK ONE | LIFE QUESTIONS

Jesus' Deity

> "Now when Jesus came into the district of Caesarea Philippi, He was asking His disciples, 'Who do people say that the Son of Man is?' And they said, 'Some say John the Baptist; and others, Elijah; but still others, Jeremiah, or one of the prophets.' He said to them, 'But who do you say that I am?' Simon Peter answered, 'You are the Christ, the Son of the living God.' And Jesus said to him, 'Blessed are you, Simon Barjona, because flesh and blood did not reveal this to you, but My Father who is in heaven.'"
>
> **MATTHEW 16:13-17**

IN GENERAL, WHAT DID JESUS' DISCIPLES BELIEVE ABOUT HIS IDENTITY?

_____

_____

_____

WHAT IS UNIQUE ABOUT PETER'S ANSWER? WHAT MIGHT HAVE PROMPTED HIM TO GIVE THAT RESPONSE?

_____

_____

_____

> "After eight days His disciples were again inside, and Thomas with them. Jesus came, the doors having been shut, and stood in their midst and said, 'Peace be with you.' Then He said to Thomas, 'Reach here with your finger, and see My hands; and reach here your hand and put it into My side; and do not be unbelieving, but believing.' Thomas answered and said to Him, 'My Lord and my God!' Jesus said to him, 'Because you have seen Me, have you believed? Blessed are they who did not see, and yet believed.'"
>
> **JOHN 20:26-29**

CHAPTER 4 | **WHO IS JESUS?**

WHAT DID THOMAS SAY ABOUT JESUS?

_____
_____
_____

HOW DID JESUS RESPOND TO THIS STATEMENT?

_____
_____
_____

> "I and the Father are one." The Jews picked up stones again to stone Him. Jesus answered them, "I showed you many good works from the Father; for which of them are you stoning Me?" The Jews answered Him, "For a good work we do not stone You, but for blasphemy; and because You, being a man, make Yourself out to be God."
>
> **JOHN 10:30-33**

WERE THE JEWS JUSTIFIED FOR BEING OFFENDED BY JESUS' WORDS? WHY OR WHY NOT?

_____
_____
_____

> "Immediately He made the disciples get into the boat and go ahead of Him to the other side, while He sent the crowds away. … And in the fourth watch of the night He came to them, walking on the sea. When the disciples saw Him walking on the sea, they were terrified, and said, 'It is a ghost!' And they cried out in fear. But immediately Jesus spoke to them, saying, 'Take courage, it is I; do not be afraid.' Peter said to Him, 'Lord, if it is You, command me to come to You on the water.' And He said, 'Come!' And Peter got out

> of the boat, and walked on the water and came toward Jesus. But seeing the wind, he became frightened, and beginning to sink, he cried out, 'Lord, save me!' Immediately Jesus stretched out His hand and took hold of him, and said to him, 'You of little faith, why did you doubt?' When they got into the boat, the wind stopped. And those who were in the boat worshiped Him, saying, 'You are certainly God's Son!'"
>
> **MATTHEW 14:22, 25-33**

WHAT EVIDENCE OF JESUS' DEITY IS PRESENTED IN THIS STORY?

_____

_____

_____

LISTEN: *THE HUMANITY AND DEITY OF CHRIST* BY KEN BOA

LISTENING NOTES

_____

_____

_____

LISTEN: *WHO IS JESUS?* BY STEPHEN DAVEY

LISTENING NOTES

_____

_____

_____

Related Resources

- *The Jesus I Never Knew*, Phillip Yancey
- *Basic Theology,* Charles Ryrie
- *The Case for Christ,* Lee Strobel
- *Cold-Case Christianity,* J. Warner Wallace

CHAPTER 4 | **WHO IS JESUS?**

The Take It Further section is to help you go a little deeper through challenging questions, audio recommendations, and reflective exercises. This section is optional for use in your study. You may do all, one, or none of the suggestions.

Take it Further

THINK: IF JESUS CLAIMED TO BE GOD, WHY DIDN'T HE DEFEND HIMSELF AGAINST MEN?

_____

_____

_____

OBERVE: WATCH THE *JESUS FILM* ON WWW.JESUSFILM.ORG

_____

_____

_____

CONSIDER:

> "Jesus of Nazareth, without money and arms, conquered more millions than Alexander the Great, Caesar, Mohammed, and Napoleon; without science and learning, he shed more light on things human and divine than all philosophers and scholars combined; without the eloquence obtained by education, he spoke such words of life as were never spoken before or since, and produced effects which lie beyond the reach of orator or poet; without writing a single line, he set more pens in motion, and furnished themes for more sermons, orations, discussions, learned volumes, works of art, and songs of praise than the whole army of great men of ancient and modern times." PHILIP SCHAFF, *German-American theologian and church historian*

LISTEN TO FERNANDO ORTEGA'S SONG *GIVE ME JESUS* SUNG BY JEREMY CAMP (YOUTUBE). HOW DO THE FACTS ABOUT JESUS CHRIST INTERSECT WITH THE LONGING OF THE SINGER'S HEART?

_____

_____

_____

_____

Notes

Chapter 5: Why Did Jesus Come?

You're interrupted by a phone call in the middle of a busy day. You and the caller exchange pleasantries and while you lament answering your phone in the first place, the caller continues to shoot the breeze. Sooner or later, you insert this question as politely as you can into the conversation: *Why did you call?* In other words, get to the point; otherwise you're wasting my time! Even if the call was simply a social connection and nothing more, it puts you at ease to know the caller's purpose.

We're skeptical about salesmen and fundraisers, more so when we suspect their undisclosed reason for calling. We're reluctant to engage with others without knowing the purpose of the connection. We're wired to ask why, which makes Jesus' statements about His purpose significant. He didn't leave the why question unanswered.

Some Say

"The Son of God became a man to enable men to become sons of God."
C.S. LEWIS, *author*

"The dying Jesus is the evidence of God's anger toward sin; but the living Jesus is the proof of God's love and forgiveness."
LORENZ EIFERT, *pastor*

To die in agony upon a cross does not create a martyr; he must first will his own execution."
HENRIK IBSEN, *Norwegian playwright*

"Jesus does not give recipes that show the way to God as other teachers of religion do. He is himself the way."
KARL BARTH, *philosopher*

> " A man who was completely innocent, offered Himself as a sacrifice for the good of others, including His enemies, and became the ransom of the world. It was a perfect act." MAHATMA GANDHI, *Indian religious and political leader*

WHAT TYPE OF PURPOSE WOULD MOTIVATE A PERSON TO DIE WILLINGLY?

_____
_____
_____
_____

No Coffin on Display

In the villages of Northern India, a missionary was preaching in a bazaar. As he closed his message, a Muslim gentleman approached him and said, "You must admit we have one thing you have not, and it is better than anything you have." The missionary smiled and said, "I should be pleased to hear what it is." The Muslim said, "You know when we go to Mecca we at least find a coffin. But when you Christians go to Jerusalem, which is your Mecca, you find nothing but an empty grave." The missionary smiled and said, "That is just the difference. Mohammed is dead; Mohammed is in the coffin….Jesus Christ, whose kingdom is to include all nations and kindreds and tribes, is not here; He is risen. And all power in heaven and on earth is given unto Him. That is our hope." (Illustration by Pastor Evie Megginson)

WHAT DIFFERENCES DO YOU NOTICE BETWEEN JESUS CHRIST AND OTHER RELIGIOUS LEADERS?

_____
_____
_____
_____

Questions to Consider

- Why did Jesus come?
- What did Jesus do?
- Why and how did Jesus die?
- Did Jesus really rise again?
- What else is left for Jesus to do?

Why Did Jesus Come?

Review these verses:

> Behold, an angel of the Lord appeared to him in a dream, saying, 'Joseph, son of David, do not be afraid to take Mary as your wife…She will bear a Son; and you shall call His name Jesus, for He will save His people from their sins.'"
>
> **MATTHEW 1:21**
>
> "So Jesus said to them again, 'Truly, truly, I say to you, I am the door of the sheep. All who came before Me are thieves and robbers, but the sheep did not hear them. I am the door; if anyone enters through Me, he will be saved, and will go in and out and find pasture. The thief comes only to steal and kill and destroy; I came that they may have life, and have it abundantly. I am the good shepherd; the good shepherd lays down His life for the sheep.'"
>
> **JOHN 10:7-11**
>
> "For the Son of Man has come to seek and to save that which was lost."
>
> **LUKE 19:10**

WHAT REASONS FOR JESUS' COMING ARE FOUND IN THESE PASSAGES?

_____

_____

_____

_____

What Did Jesus Do?

- He began His ministry by being hungry, yet He is the Bread of Life **11:14-20**
- Jesus ended His earthly ministry by being thirsty, yet He is the Living Water. **JOHN 4:15-16**
- Jesus was weary, yet He is our rest. **MATTHEW 11:28-30**
- Jesus paid tribute, yet He is the King. **MATTHEW 22:15-22**
- Jesus was accused of having a demon, yet He cast out demons. **LUKE 11:14-20**
- Jesus wept, yet He wipes away our tears. **JOHN 11:35; REVELATION 21:4**
- Jesus was sold for thirty pieces of silver, yet He redeemed the world. **MATTHEW 27:3-4**
- Jesus was brought as a lamb to the slaughter, yet He is the Good Shepherd **ISAIAH 53:7**
- Jesus died, yet by His death He destroyed the power of death. **1 CORINTHIANS 15:56-57**

Gregory of Nazianzus, A.D. 381

Even the greatest skeptic would agree that Jesus altered history dramatically. Consider these accomplishments:

- Led an exemplary life that millions have imitated.
- Provided the most influential teachings of all time.
- Offered hope to the most unfortunate outcasts.

According to Scripture, Jesus demonstrated power over disease, nature, and even death.

POWER OVER DISEASE:	POWER OVER NATURE:	POWER OVER DEATH:
A leper	Water to wine	The widow's son
A paralytic	Quieted storm	Jairus' daughter
Nobleman's son	Huge fishing catch	Lazarus, a friend
Withered hand	Walked on water	Resurrection

WHY DO YOU THINK JESUS PERFORMED SUCH A WIDE VARIETY OF MIRACLES?

_____
_____
_____
_____

WHICH ONES ARE THE MOST SIGNIFICANT TO YOU?

_____
_____
_____
_____

> "If I do not do the works of My Father, do not believe Me; but if I do them, though you do not believe Me, believe the works, so that you may know and understand that the Father is in Me, and I in the Father."
>
> **JOHN 10:37-38**
>
> "For I have come down from heaven, not to do My own will, but the will of Him who sent Me. This is the will of Him who sent Me, that of all that He has given Me I lose nothing, but raise it up on the last day. For this is the will of My Father, that everyone who beholds the Son and believes in Him will have eternal life, and I Myself will raise him up on the last day."
>
> **JOHN 6:38-40**

ACCORDING TO THE ABOVE PASSAGES, WHAT WAS JESUS' PURPOSE FOR PERFORMING MIRACLES?

_____
_____
_____
_____

CHAPTER 5 | **WHY DID JESUS COME?**

Why and How Did Jesus Die?

- But He was pierced through for our transgressions, He was crushed for our iniquities; the chastening for our well-being fell upon Him, and by His scourging we are healed. All of us like sheep have gone astray, each of us has turned to his own way; but the Lord has caused the iniquity of us all to fall on Him." **ISAIAH 53:5-6**

- " ...for all have sinned and fall short of the glory of God, and are justified freely by his grace through the redemption that came by Christ Jesus." **ROMANS 3:23-24**

- "But God demonstrates his own love for us in this: While we were still sinners, Christ died for us." **ROMANS 5:8**

WHAT IS THE CONNECTION BETWEEN GOD'S LOVE AND JESUS' DEATH?

_____
_____
_____
_____
_____

Death by Crucifixion

Crucifixion was a Roman method of execution reserved for slaves, foreigners and criminals. Roman citizens (such as the Apostle Paul) by law could not be subjected to this brutal, sadistic punishment. Crucifixion often meant days of excruciating pain before death finally came. Like other popular means of execution and torture throughout history, a crucifixion usually drew a crowd of bystanders.

> "At that time two robbers were crucified with Him, one on the right and one on the left."
> **MATTHEW 27:38**

WHAT IS THE SIGNIFICANCE OF THE METHOD OF JESUS' DEATH, CRUCIFIXION?

_____
_____
_____
_____
_____
_____

CHAPTER 5 | **WHY DID JESUS COME?**

Did Jesus Really Rise Again?

It's one thing to believe that Jesus actually lived. It's another to believe He performed miracles and was killed by Roman authorities in Jerusalem. **But to believe that He actually rose from the dead is the most significant step of all**. And yet, if Jesus was not resurrected, then all of Christianity is a hoax, and all of His followers throughout the history of the church until now have been deceived. The resurrection is the crux of Christianity. For this reason, the Bible carefully demonstrates that many witnesses saw Jesus after death and burial. Paul makes the case in the verse

> "The resurrection of Christ is the linchpin of our Christian faith." LON SOLOMON

> "For I delivered to you as of first importance what I also received, that Christ died for our sins according to the Scriptures, and that He was buried, and that He was raised on the third day according to the Scriptures, and that He appeared to Cephas, then to the twelve. After that He appeared to more than five hundred brethren at one time, most of whom remain until now, but some have fallen asleep; then He appeared to James, then to all the apostles; and last of all, as to one untimely born, He appeared to me also."
>
> **1 CORINTHIANS 15:3-8**

ACCORDING TO THIS PASSAGE, HOW STRONG WAS THE EVIDENCE TO PROVE JESUS' RESURRECTION? CONSIDERING THE TECHNOLOGY OF THE TIME, WHAT WAS THE SIGNIFICANCE OF HAVING EYEWITNESSES?

_____

_____

_____

_____

The truth of the resurrection assures us of our salvation and gives hope to all who believe in our future resurrection from the dead. Instead, we have all of these things because of the reality of the resurrection. We have a glorious hope because of our faith in the living Savior. (Adapted from Charles Ryrie's Basic Theology)

- "You killed the author of life, but God raised him from the dead. We are witnesses of this." **Acts 3:15**

- "Jesus answered them, 'Destroy this temple, and I will raise it again in three days.' The Jews replied, 'It has taken forty-six years to build this temple, and you are going to raise it in three days?' But the temple he had spoken of was his body. After he was raised from the dead, his disciples recalled what he had said. Then they believed the Scripture and the words that Jesus had spoken." **John 2:19-22**

- "And if Christ has not been raised, your faith is futile; you are still in your sins." **1 Corinthians 15:17**

ACCORDING TO THE VERSES ABOVE, WHY IS CHRIST'S RESURRECTION SO IMPORTANT?

_____

_____

_____

When Jesus was taken away to die, His small handful of followers scattered and hid. Within a few years, the Christian faith had permeated no less than the Roman Empire, and those original followers had become willing to face execution themselves.

HOW CAN WE ACCOUNT FOR THESE OCCURRENCES WITHOUT A WELL-ATTESTED RESURRECTION?

_____

_____

_____

CHAPTER 5 | **WHY DID JESUS COME?**

What Else Is Left for Jesus to Do?

"According to the Lord's own word, we tell you that we who are still alive, who are left till the coming of the Lord, will certainly not precede those who have fallen asleep. For the Lord himself will come down from heaven, with a loud command, with the voice of the archangel and with the trumpet call of God, and the dead in Christ will rise first. After that, we who are still alive and are left will be caught up together with them in the clouds to meet the Lord in the air. And so we will be with the Lord forever. Therefore encourage each other with these words." **Thessalonians 4:15-18**

> "There exists no document from the ancient world witnessed by so excellent a set of textual and historical testimonies, and offering so superb an array of historical data on which the intelligent decision may be made. Skepticism regarding the historical credentials of Christianity is based upon an irrational bias."
> CLARK PINNOCK, *Professor, McMasters University, Toronto*

- "Behold, I am coming soon! My reward is with me, and I will give to everyone according to what he has done." **Revelation 22:12**

- "And after He had said these things, He was lifted up while they were looking on, and a cloud received Him out of their sight. And as they were gazing intently into the sky while He was going, behold, two men in white clothing stood beside them. They also said, 'Men of Galilee, why do you stand looking into the sky? This Jesus, who has been taken up from you into heaven, will come in just the same way as you have watched Him go into heaven.'" **Acts 1:9-11**

WHAT ENCOURAGEMENT DID THE ANGELS OFFER THE DISCIPLES?

_____
_____
_____
_____

LISTEN: *OUT OF THE GRAVE* BY CRAWFORD LORITTS

LISTENING NOTES
_____
_____
_____
_____
_____
_____
_____
_____
_____
_____

Related Resources

- *The Jesus I Never Knew*, Phillip Yancey
- *Basic Theology,* Charles Ryrie
- *The Case for Christ,* Lee Strobel
- *Cold-Case Christianity,* J. Warner Wallace

CHAPTER 5 | **WHY DID JESUS COME?**

> *The Take It Further section is to help you go a little deeper through challenging questions, audio recommendations, and reflective exercises. This section is optional for use in your study. You may do all, one, or none of the suggestions.*

Take it Further

THINK: DO FEEL IT WAS NECESSARY FOR JESUS TO DIE? WHY OR WHY NOT?

_____
_____
_____
_____
_____

OBSERVE: WATCH *THE PASSION OF THE CHRIST* FILM. COMPARE THE "END" OF JESUS' LIFE ON EARTH WITH OTHER MAJOR RELIGIOUS FIGURES: GANDHI, MOHAMMED, BUDDHA, THE MANY HINDU GODS, CONFUCIOUS, BRIGHAM YOUNG, MARY BAKER EDDY, ETC.

CONSIDER: WHE WE THINK ABOUT DEATH, WE TEND TO THINK OF AN END. HOW WAS JESUS' DEATH A BEGINNING INSTEAD?

_____
_____
_____
_____
_____

Notes

Chapter 6: Can I Be Accepted and Forgiven?

— Some Say —

"Karl Menninger, the famed psychiatrist, once said that if he could convince the patients in psychiatric hospitals that their sins were forgiven, 75 percent of them could walk out the next day!"
Today in the Word, March 1989, p. 8

"There is no love without forgiveness, and there is no forgiveness without love."
BRYANT H. MCGILL, *American poet and author*

"Anger makes you smaller, while forgiveness forces you to grow beyond what you were."
CHERIE CARTER-SCOTT, *author, life coach and motivational speaker*

"Resentment is like a glass of poison that a man drinks; then he sits down and waits for his enemy to die."
UNKNOWN

After you answer the following question, consider the power of forgiveness in the next two stories.

WHY IS FORGIVENESS SO IMPORTANT TO THE HUMAN EXPERIENCE?

_____

_____

_____

_____

Story 1: Jody and Chip Ferlaak

After church on July 29, 2001, Jody and Chip Ferlaak took their three young children to a Sunday brunch at a popular restaurant. Within minutes of sitting down with their food, a woman named Cindy, 38, attempted suicide by crashing her car into the restaurant's front door. All the family were injured along with 6 other adults and children. Teagan Ferlaak, 4, died on impact.

When the incident went to court, Chip and Jody pushed through their emotional turmoil to speak to everyone in the courtroom. They forgave Cindy. Jody said, "I felt so cheated out of Teagan's life, there was a part of me that wanted to see this woman get what she deserved. But it was almost like God said, 'I can't and won't let you do it.'"

In court, they described how much damage their family had suffered, but that they wished Cindy to become a better person in the end. She should go on living. Chip said, "When you truly forgive someone, you can go on living your life."

> "He that cannot forgive others breaks the bridge over which he must pass himself; for every man has need to be forgiven."
> THOMAS FULLER, *English clergyman*

Story 2: Ernest Gordon's Miracle on the River Kwai

The behavior of the Scottish soldiers, forced by their Japanese captors to labor on a jungle railroad, had degenerated into vicious barbarism. But one afternoon something happened. The officer in charge became enraged because a shovel was missing. He demanded that the missing shovel be produced, or else. When nobody in the squadron budged, the officer got his gun and threatened to kill them all on the spot. It was obvious the officer meant business. Finally, one of the Scottish captives stepped forward.

The officer put away his gun, picked up a shovel, and beat the man to death. When it was over, the survivors picked up the bloody corpse and carried it with them to the second tool check. This time, no shovel was missing. Indeed, there had been a miscount at the first check point. Word of the miscount and the subsequent beating spread like wildfire through the whole camp. An innocent man had been willing to die to save the others! The incident had a profound effect on the prisoners. The men began to treat each other like brothers. When the Allies swept in to rescue them, the survivors, physically not much more than human skeletons, lined up in front of their captors and insisted: "No more hatred. No more killing. Now what we need is forgiveness." Sacrificial love had that much transforming power.

WHY DOES FORGIVENESS TRIGGER SUCH A POWERFUL RESPONSE IN PEOPLE?

_____

_____

_____

_____

CHAPTER 6 | **CAN I BE ACCEPTED AND FORGIVEN?**

Making Forgiveness Personal

HAVE YOU EVER HAD AN EXPERIENCE OF FORGIVING SOMEONE WHO HAS NEVER ASKED FOR IT? DESCRIBE.

_____
_____
_____
_____
_____
_____
_____

WHAT EMOTIONS ARE INVOLVED WHEN SOMEONE FORGIVES YOU?

_____
_____
_____
_____
_____
_____
_____

WHAT EMOTIONS ARE INVOLVED WHEN YOU ARE THE ONE GRANTING FORGIVENESS?

_____
_____
_____
_____
_____
_____
_____
_____

BASED ON YOUR THOUGHTS, GIVE A SIMPLE DEFINITION OF FORGIVENESS.

_____
_____
_____
_____
_____
_____
_____

CHAPTER 6 | **CAN I BE ACCEPTED AND FORGIVEN?**

But Am I Really All That Bad?

Most individuals think of themselves as generally good people who happen to mess up every once in a while. After all, nobody is perfect, right? Let's look at what Jesus has to say about this idea. Read **Matthew 5:21-28** and answer the following questions:

> "You have heard that the ancients were told, 'You shall not commit murder' and 'Whoever commits murder shall be liable to the court.' But I say to you that everyone who is angry with his brother shall be guilty before the court; and whoever says to his brother, 'You good-for-nothing,' shall be guilty before the supreme court; and whoever says, 'You fool,' shall be guilty enough to go into the fiery hell. Therefore if you are presenting your offering at the altar, and there remember that your brother has something against you, leave your offering there before the altar and go; first be reconciled to your brother, and then come and present your offering. Make friends quickly with your opponent at law while you are with him on the way, so that your opponent may not hand you over to the judge, and the judge to the officer, and you be thrown into prison. Truly I say to you, you will not come out of there until you have paid up the last cent. You have heard that it was said, 'You shall not commit adultery'; but I say to you that everyone who looks at a woman with lust for her has already committed adultery with her in his heart."
>
> **Matthew 5:21-28**

WHAT WRONG BEHAVIORS DOES JESUS REFERENCE?

_____
_____
_____
_____
_____

IS JESUS PRIMARILY CONCERNED WITH ACTIONS OR DOES HE EXPRESS A DEEPER CONCERN?

_____

_____

_____

_____

_____

_____

_____

WHY MIGHT GOD BE SO CONCERNED WITH OUR THOUGHT LIFE?

_____

_____

_____

_____

_____

_____

_____

IF YOU MEASURED YOURSELF BY THE SAME STANDARD OF RIGHT AND WRONG JESUS GIVES US IN **Matthew 5,** HOW WOULD YOU FARE?

___

___

___

___

___

___

___

___

HOW HAS THIS PASSAGE HELPED DEVELOP YOUR UNDERSTANDING OF OUR HUMAN PROBLEM, AND HOW HAS IT INFLUENCED YOUR PERCEIVED NEED FOR FORGIVENESS?

___

___

___

___

___

___

___

___

Do We Need Forgiveness?

It's human nature to evaluate using a relative scale. Instead of measuring our overall standing, we compare ourselves to others near us. When it comes to human performance, success is more a matter of comparison than achieving actual perfection. Perhaps that's because absolute perfection is so unattainable. Is that the standard of the Bible: just do a little bit better than the next guy?

> "You, therefore, have no excuse, you who pass judgment on someone else, for at whatever point you judge the other, you are condemning yourself, because you who pass judgment do the same things."
> **ROMANS 2:1**

EXPLAIN THE STANDARD DESCRIBED IN THIS PASSAGE.

_____
_____
_____
_____
_____
_____
_____
_____
_____

CHAPTER 6 | CAN I BE ACCEPTED AND FORGIVEN?

What Is the Basis for God's Forgiveness?

WHAT ARE SOME OF THE WAYS WE TRY TO "MAKE UP" FOR OUR OFFENSES?

_____
_____
_____
_____
_____
_____
_____
_____

HOW IS THIS DIFFERENT FROM ASKING FORGIVENESS?

_____
_____
_____
_____
_____
_____
_____
_____

In this world, we are rewarded based on our effort. It's a principle instilled in us from earliest childhood. We earn approval, allowance, school grades, respect, salary, and so on. It's no wonder we think we can earn God's acceptance. Not even doing good works, being baptized, being born into a Christian family, joining a church or even recycling can win God's approval.

HAVE YOU EVER TRIED TO EARN GOD'S APPROVAL? EXPLAIN.

_____
_____
_____
_____
_____
_____
_____
_____

CHAPTER 6 | **CAN I BE ACCEPTED AND FORGIVEN?**

The following verses tell a story of how we come into a relationship with God.

- "For all have sinned and fall short of the glory of God." **Romans 3:23**

- "For the wages of sin is death, but the free gift of God is eternal life in Christ Jesus our Lord." **Romans 6:23**

- "But God demonstrates His own love toward us, in that while we were yet sinners, Christ died for us." **Romans 5:8**

- "That if you confess with your mouth Jesus as Lord, and believe in your heart that God raised Him from the dead, you will be saved." **Romans 10:9**

- "If we confess our sins, He is faithful and righteous to forgive us our sins and to cleanse us from all unrighteousness." **1 John 1:9**

ACCORDING TO THE VERSES ABOVE, WHAT IS THE BASIS OF GOD'S FORGIVENESS?

_____
_____
_____
_____
_____

ACCORDING TO THE VERSES, WHAT IS OUR PART?

_____
_____
_____
_____
_____
_____
_____

In the last chapter we discussed the death and resurrection of Jesus. We also read the prophecy given about Jesus in **Isaiah 53:5** which says: *"But He was pierced through for our transgressions, He was crushed for our iniquities; the chastening for our well-being fell upon Him, and by His scourging we are healed."* Sometimes it can hard to understand why Jesus had to suffer because of us.

WHAT DOES Isaiah 53:5 IMPLY ABOUT THE SERIOUSNESS OF OUR WRONG ACTIONS (TRANSGRESSIONS, INIQUITIES)?

_____
_____
_____
_____
_____
_____
_____

CHAPTER 6 | **CAN I BE ACCEPTED AND FORGIVEN?**

HOW DOES IT MAKE YOU FEEL TO KNOW THAT JESUS SUFFERED INTENSELY BECAUSE OF THE WRONG THINGS YOU HAVE DONE?

_____

_____

_____

_____

_____

Redemption means: "to buy back."

Scripture gives us a consistent picture: our disobedience earned the penalty of death, but God refused to abandon us. Instead, He allowed His Son, obedient and perfect, to take the punishment reserved for us. Jesus received our just due, and we received His: a wonderful place in God's family—a once and for all reunion with our Divine Father. We need never be lost again.

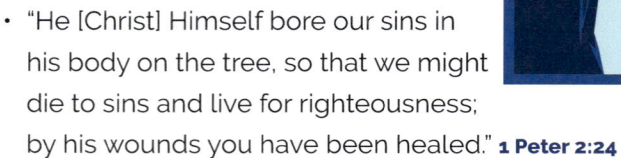

- "He [Christ] Himself bore our sins in his body on the tree, so that we might die to sins and live for righteousness; by his wounds you have been healed." **1 Peter 2:24**

- "...in whom we have redemption, the forgiveness of sins." **Colossians 1:14**

- "When you were dead in your transgressions and the uncircumcision of your flesh, He made you alive together with Him, having forgiven us all our transgressions, having canceled out the certificate of debt consisting of decrees against us, which was hostile to us; and He has taken it out of the way, having nailed it to the cross." **Colossians 2:13-14**

- "Jesus said to him, 'I am the way, the truth and the life; no one comes to the Father except through Me." **John 14:6**

RESTATE IN YOUR OWN WORDS HOW CAN ONE RECEIVE THIS FORGIVENESS?

_____
_____
_____
_____
_____
_____
_____

Read the passage below:

> "But if we walk in the Light as He Himself is in the Light, we have fellowship with one another, and the blood of Jesus His Son cleanses us from all sin. If we say that we have no sin, we are deceiving ourselves and the truth is not in us. If we confess our sins, He is faithful and righteous to forgive us our sins and to cleanse us from all unrighteousness."
>
> **1 John 1:7-9**

WHAT CENTRAL IDEAS ARE CONVEYED BY THE KEY WORDS?

_____
_____
_____
_____
_____
_____
_____

CHAPTER 6 | **CAN I BE ACCEPTED AND FORGIVEN?**

WHAT DO THESE IDEAS SUGGEST ABOUT HOW WE RECEIVE GOD'S FORGIVENESS?

WHAT IS THE RESULT OF FORGIVENESS?

> "Truly, truly, I say to you, he who hears My word, and believes Him who sent Me, has eternal life, and does not come into judgment, but has passed out of death into life."
>
> **John 5:24**

> "Therefore, since we have been justified through faith, we have peace with God through our Lord Jesus Christ."
>
> **Romans 5:1**

WHAT IS MEANT BY CROSSING OVER FROM DEATH TO LIFE? IS THIS LITERAL OR METAPHORICAL? EXPLAIN.

_____
_____
_____
_____
_____

WHY IS PEACE NAMED AS THE ULTIMATE RESULT OF BEING FORGIVEN BY GOD? EXPLAIN.

_____
_____
_____
_____
_____

CHAPTER 6 | **CAN I BE ACCEPTED AND FORGIVEN?**

What is faith? Faith isn't an intellectual understanding or mental assent. Faith is not a feeling. Instead, faith is a choice and it involves your mind and your will. Faith demands action.

> "That if you confess with your mouth Jesus as Lord, and believe in your heart that God raised Him from the dead, you will be saved."
> **Romans 10:9**

WOULD YOU LIKE TO MAKE A CHOICE TODAY TO ADMIT YOU'RE A SINNER, BELIEVE JESUS CHRIST AS GOD AND CONFESS THAT HE ALONE IS ENOUGH FOR SALVATION?

_____

_____

_____

_____

_____

If you're ready, you can pray a prayer similar to this:

Heavenly Father,

Today, I am admitting that I am a sinner and my sin separates me from You, a holy and righteous God. I turn away from my sin and I repent. Thank You for forgiving all my sins. I believe that You have paid the penalty for my sin on the cross and that You rose again from the dead to offer me new life. I commit my life to You and put my trust in Your Son, Jesus Christ. Amen.

IF YOU HAVE QUESTIONS ABOUT SALVATION OR WOULD LIKE TO DISCUSS THIS DECISION WITH SOMEONE, WE ENCOURAGE YOU TO TALK WITH YOUR PAUL.

_____

_____

_____

_____

_____

LISTEN: *SOLA FIDE: THE GREAT DIVIDE* BY STEPHEN DAVEY

LISTENING NOTES

Related Resources

- *Son of God*, movie

The Take It Further section is to help you go a little deeper through challenging questions, audio recommendations, and reflective exercises. This section is optional for use in your study. You may do all, one, or none of the suggestions.

Take it Further

THINK: DOES BEING "GOOD" ENHANCE OUR ABILITY TO RECEIVE GOD'S FORGIVENESS?

_____
_____
_____
_____
_____

OBSERVE: WATCH THE FILM *LUTHER*. WHEN MARTIN LUTHER FIRST UNDERSTOOD GRACE, HOW DID HIS LIFE CHANGE? HOW WAS THE WORLD IMPACTED BY HIS PERSONAL EXPERIENCE OF FORGIVENESS?

_____
_____
_____
_____
_____

CONSIDER: WHAT HAS BEEN YOUR PERSONAL EXPERIENCE WITH JESUS CHRIST? HOW WOULD YOU DESCRIBE YOUR RELATIONSHIP WITH HIM TODAY?

_____
_____
_____
_____
_____
_____
_____
_____

LISTEN TO AND DISCUSS *CHANGE THE WORLD (LOST ONES)* BY ANBERLIN OR *ALL I NEED IS EVERYTHING* BY OVER THE RHINE.

_____
_____
_____
_____
_____
_____
_____
_____

CHAPTER 6 | **CAN I BE ACCEPTED AND FORGIVEN?**

Notes

The OPERATION TIMOTHY GLOBAL Book Series
Available on Amazon

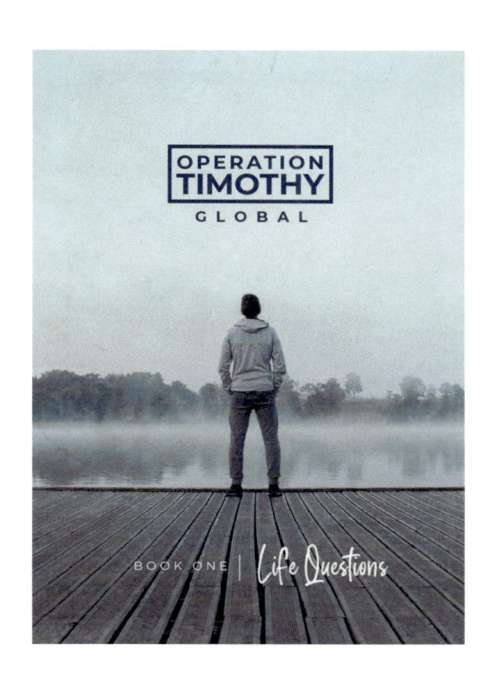

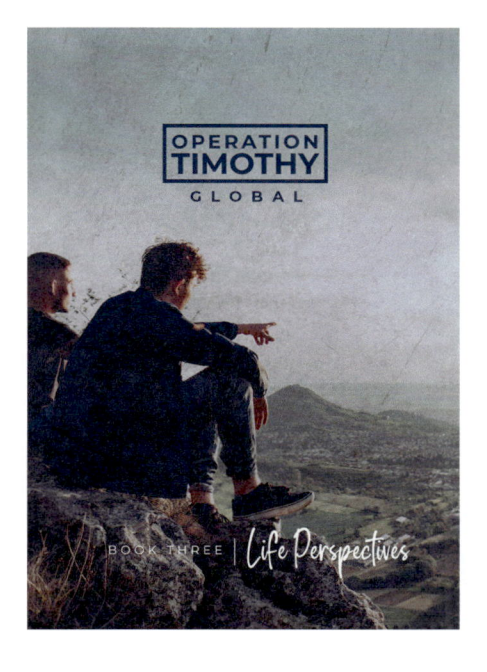

- Book One | Life Questions
- Book Two | Life Foundations
- Book Three | Life Perspectives
- Leader's Guide

Made in the USA
Columbia, SC
12 April 2025